ROYAL COURT

Royal Court Theatre presents

PRESENCE

by David Harrower

First performance at the Royal Court Jerwood Theatre Upstairs,
Sloane Square, London on 19 April 2001.

Sponsored by the Jerwood Charitable Foundation

JERWOOD
NEW PLAYWRIGHTS

D0320132

PRESENCE

by **David Harrower**

Cast in order of appearance
George **Ralf Little**
Paul **William Ash**
Pete **Michael Legge**
Marian **Sarah Woodward**
Elke **Christine Tremarco**

Director **James Kerr**
Designer **Rae Smith**
Lighting Designer **Paule Constable**
Sound Designer **Fergus O'Hare for Aura**
Assistant Director **Nina Raine**
Casting Director **Lisa Makin**
Production Manager **Sue Bird**
Company Stage Manager **Cath Binks**
Stage Management **Pea Horsley, Sharon Cooper**
Stage Management Work Placement **Karolina Norgate**
Costume Supervisor **Iona Kenrick**
Company Voice Work **Patsy Rodenburg**

Royal Court Theatre would like to thank the following for their help with this production:
Wardrobe care by Persil and Comfort courtesy of Lever Brothers Ltd.

JERWOOD
NEW PLAYWRIGHTS

Since 1993 Jerwood New Playwrights have contributed to some of the Royal Court's most successful productions, including SHOPPING AND FUCKING by Mark Ravenhill (co-production with Out of Joint), EAST IS EAST by Ayub Khan-Din (co-production with Tamasha), THE BEAUTY QUEEN OF LEENANE by Martin McDonagh (co-production with Druid Theatre Company), THE WEIR by Conor McPherson, REAL CLASSY AFFAIR by Nick Grosso and THE FORCE OF CHANGE by Gary Mitchell, ON RAFTERY'S HILL by Marina Carr (co-production with Druid Theatre Company),4.48 PSYCHOSIS by Sarah Kane and UNDER THE BLUE SKY by David Eldridge.

The Jerwood Charitable Foundation is a registered charity dedicated to imaginative and responsible funding and sponsorship of the arts, education, design and other areas of human endeavour and excellence. This season Jerwood New Playwrights are supporting PRESENCE by David Harrower, HERONS by Simon Stephens and CLUBLAND by Roy Williams.

www.jerwood.org.uk

UNDER THE BLUE SKY by David Eldridge
(photo: Ivan Kyncl)

EAST IS EAST by Ayub Khan-Din
(photo: Robert Day)

THE COMPANY

David Harrower (writer)
Theatre includes: Knives in Hens (Traverse/Bush);
Kill the Old Torture Their Young (Traverse).
Adaptations include: The Chrysalids (RNT/ BT
Connections), Six Characters in Search of an
Author, (Young Vic), Woyzeck (Royal Lyceum,
Edinburgh).
Radio includes: 54% Acrylic (Radio 4).
Awards include: German Critics Award for Best
Foreign Play for Knives in Hens and 1999 Meyer-
Whitworth Award for Kill the Old Torture Their
Young.

William Ash
Theatre includes: Juno and the Paycock (Donmar
Warehouse); View from the Bridge (I.I.T.C).
Television includes: Sherlock Holmes, How We
Used to Live, Making Out, Children's Ward,
Heartbeat, Soldier Soldier, Bare Necessities, Beck,
Born to Run, Where The Heart Is, Anorak of Fire,
All the King's Men, Frightmares, Clocking Off.
Film includes: Mad About Mambo, Fanny and Elvis.

Paule Constable (lighting designer)
For the Royal Court: Credible Witness, The
Country, Dublin Carol, The Weir, The Glory of
Living.
Other theatre includes: The Seagull, Tales from
Ovid, The Dispute, Uncle Vanya, Beckett Shorts,
The Mysteries (RSC); The Villains' Opera, Darker
Face of the Earth, Haroun and the Sea of Stories,
Caucasian Chalk Circle (RNT); Amadeus (West
End, Broadway, Olivier nomination); Les Miserables
(Tel Aviv); The Servant (Lyric); More Grimms' Tales
(Young Vic and New York); four productions for
Theatre de Complicite including the Olivier
nominated Street of Crocodiles.
Opera includes: productions for the English
National Opera, Welsh National Opera, Scottish
Opera, Opera North, Glyndebourne, La Monnaie.

James Kerr (director)
Currently Associate Director of Liverpool
Theatres. Director on attachment at the RNT
Studio, 1997.
Theatre includes: The Arbor, Don Juan, Ajax, Man
of Mode, La Tete sur les Eparles (RNT Studio);
Twelfth Night (Liverpool Playhouse); Dealer's
Choice (West Yorkshire Playhouse); Suppliants
(Gate); Morphic Resonance (Donmar Warehouse);
The Recruiting Officer (Chichester Festival
Theatre); The Darker Face of the Earth (RNT).

Michael Legge
Theatre includes: Cressida (Albery).
Television includes: The Precious Blood.
Film includes: Whatever Happened to Harold
Smith, Angela's Ashes, Stray Dogs, Soft Sand
Blue Sea.
Michael was nominated Best Newcomer by
the London Film Critics' Circle for Angela's
Ashes.

Ralf Little
Theatre includes: Love on the Dole (RNT).
Television includes: Aladdin, Two Pints of
Lager and a Packet of Crisps, The Royle
Family, Always and Everyone, Flint Street
Nativity, Bostock's Cup, The Ward,
Heartbeat, Sloggers.
Film includes: 24 Hour Party People, Al's
Lads, Harry on the Boat.

Fergus O'Hare (sound designer)
For the Royal Court: Credible Witness,
Backpay, One More Wasted Year, Bazaar,
Stranger's House.
Other theatre includes: Twelfth Night
(Liverpool Playhouse); Conversations After a
Burial, Cressida, Bash, Our Father, The Jew of
Malta (Almeida); Volpone (RSC); Noises Off,
The Merchant of Venice, Money, An Enemy of
the People, Guiding Star (RNT); Pera Palas,
The Odyssey (Gate); John Diamond, A Lump
in the Throat (Grace); Orpheus Descending,
Merrily We Roll Along, Passion Play (also West
End), Juno and the Paycock, The Life of Stuff,
Playland, Glengarry Glen Ross, True West,
Endgame, Habeas Corpus, The Bullet, How I
Learned to Drive, Electra (also Broadway)
(Donmar Warehouse); Macbeth (Queen's);
Arabian Nights (Young Vic); The Snowman
(The Peacock); Starstruck (Tricycle); Yard,
Breaking In (Bush); The Death of Cool, By
Many Wounds (Hampstead); Dancing at
Lughnasa (National Youth Theatre); Pippin,
The Golem (Bridewell); Edna-The Spectacle
(Haymarket).

Nina Raine (assistant director)
For the Royal Court: Mouth To Mouth, Far Away, My Zinc Bed.
Theatre includes: Passion Play, Miss Julie (Burton Taylor Theatre, Oxford); The Way of the World (for the Red Cross at Trebinshwyn); Ashes to Ashes.
Nina is currently on the Regional Theatre Young Director Scheme at the Royal Court Theatre.

Rae Smith (designer)
For the Royal Court: Dublin Carol, The Weir (and Broadway), Some Voices, Trust.
Other theatre includes: The Servant (for Neil, Bartlett), Pinocchio, The White Devil, Cause Celebre, Sarasine, Mrs Warren's Profession, A Christmas Carol, The Letter (Lyric Hammersmith); Godspell (Chichester Theatre); The Cocktail Party, A Midsummer Night's Dream (Lyceum, Edinburgh); Endgame, Juno and the Paycock (Donmar Warehouse/Grammercy, New York); The Way of the World, Charley's Aunt (Royal Exchange, Manchester); Silence, Silence, Silence (Mladinsko Theatre, Slovenia); The Phoenician Women, Henry VI (RSC); Gormenghast (David Glass Ensemble); Death of a Salesman (West Yorkshire Playhouse); The Visit, Help I'm Alive, Ave Maria, The Street of Crocodiles, Wiseguy Scapino (Theatre de Complicite).
Opera includes: La Finta Semplice (Royal Opera House Studio); The Turn of the Screw (Brighton Festival); Don Giovanni (Welsh National Opera); The Magic Flute (Opera North); Shameless (Opera Circus); The Maids (Lyric Hammersmith).
Rae has also directed and designed Lucky (David Glass Ensemble); Mysteria (RSC) and The Terminatrix (National Theatre Studio/ENO).
She has received two design awards for working sabbaticals in Indonesia and Japan.
(website: www.rae-smith.co.uk)

Christine Tremarco
Television includes: Night and Day, Pretending to be Judith, Dance, Dockers, Clocking Off, Liverpool One, Trial and Retribution, City Central.
Film includes: The Romeo Error, Hold Back the Night, Family Ties, Face, Under The Skin, Bordertown, Priest, The Leaving of Liverpool.

Sarah Woodward
For the Royal Court: Built on Sand.
Other theatre includes: The Real Thing (Albery/Broadway); Tom and Clem (Aldwych); Habeas Corpus, Tell Me Honestly (Donmar Warehouse); Wild Oats, The Sea (RNT); Love's Labour Lost, Venetian Twins, The Tempest, Richard III, Red Noses, Camille, Love's Labour Lost, Henry V, Hamlet, Murder in the Cathedral (RSC); London Assurance (Chichester Festival/Haymarket); Kean (Old Vic); Schism in England (RNT Studio); Artist Descending a Staircase (King's Head/Duke of York); Rape of Lucrece (Almeida); Angelus, From Morning to Midnight (Soho Poly); Talk of the Devil (Bristol Old Vic); Arms and the Man, Romeo & Juliet (Regent's Park Open Air Theatre); The Winter's Tale, Charley's Aunt (Birmingham Rep); The Room, Derek, Downchild, Doom Doom Doom Doom (RSC Festival/Newcastle/Almeida).
Television includes: The Inspector Pitt Mysteries, Casualty, Poirot - Death in the Clouds, Sherlock Holmes, The Bill, The Two of Us, Gems.
Awards: nominated for a Tony Award for her role in The Real Thing and won an Olivier Best Supporting Actress Award for Tom and Clem (1998).

THE ENGLISH STAGE COMPANY AT THE ROYAL COURT

The English Stage Company at the Royal Court opened in 1956 as a subsidised theatre producing new British plays, international plays and some classical revivals.

The first artistic director George Devine aimed to create a writers' theatre, 'a place where the dramatist is acknowledged as the fundamental creative force in the theatre and where the play is more important than the actors, the director, the designer'. The urgent need was to find a contemporary style in which the play, the acting, direction and design are all combined. He believed that 'the battle will be a long one to continue to create the right conditions for writers to work in'.

Devine aimed to discover 'hard-hitting, uncompromising writers whose plays are stimulating, provocative and exciting'. The Royal Court production of John Osborne's Look Back in Anger in May 1956 is now seen as the decisive starting point of modern British drama, and the policy created a new generation of British playwrights. The first wave included John Osborne, Arnold Wesker, John Arden, Ann Jellicoe, N F Simpson and Edward Bond. Early seasons included new international plays by Bertolt Brecht, Eugène Ionesco, Samuel Beckett, Jean-Paul Sartre and Marguerite Duras.

The theatre started with the 400-seat proscenium arch Theatre Downstairs, and then in 1969 opened a second theatre, the 60-seat studio Theatre Upstairs. Productions in the Theatre Upstairs have transferred to the West End, such as Caryl Churchill's Far Away, Conor McPherson's The Weir, Kevin Elyot's My Night With Reg and Ariel Dorfman's Death and the Maiden. The Royal Court also co-produces plays which have transferred to the West End or toured internationally, such as Sebastian Barry's The Steward of Christendom and Mark Ravenhill's Shopping and Fucking (with Out of Joint), Martin McDonagh's The Beauty Queen Of Leenane (with Druid Theatre Company), Ayub Khan-Din's East is East (with Tamasha Theatre Company, and now a feature film).

Since 1994 the Royal Court's artistic policy has again been vigorously directed to finding and producing a new generation of playwrights. The writers include Joe Penhall, Rebecca Prichard, Michael Wynne, Nick Grosso, Judy Upton, Meredith Oakes, Sarah Kane, Anthony Neilson, Judith Johnson, James Stock, Jez Butterworth, Marina Carr, Simon Block, Martin McDonagh, Mark Ravenhill, Ayub Khan-Din, Tamantha Hammerschlag, Jess Walters, Che Walker, Conor McPherson, Simon Stephens, Richard Bean, Roy

photo: Andy Chopping

Williams, Gary Mitchell, Mick Mahoney, Rebecca Gilman, Christopher Shinn, Kia Corthron, David Gieselmann, Marius von Mayenburg and David Eldridge. This expanded programme of new plays has been made possible through the support of A.S.K Theater Projects, the Jerwood Charitable Foundation, the American Friends of the Royal Court Theatre and many in association with the Royal National Theatre Studio.

In recent years there have been record-breaking productions at the box office, with capacity houses for Jez Butterworth's Mojo, Sebastian Barry's The Steward of Christendom, Martin McDonagh's The Beauty Queen of Leenane, Ayub Khan-Din's East is East, Eugène Ionesco's The Chairs, David Hare's My Zinc Bed and Conor McPherson's The Weir, which transferred to the West End in October 1998 and ran for nearly two years at the Duke of York's Theatre.

The newly refurbished theatre in Sloane Square opened in February 2000, with a policy still inspired by the first artistic director George Devine. The Royal Court is an international theatre for new plays and new playwrights, and the work shapes contemporary drama in Britain and overseas.

REBUILDING THE ROYAL COURT

In 1995, the Royal Court was awarded a National Lottery grant through the Arts Council of England, to pay for three quarters of a £26m project to completely rebuild our 100-year old home. The rules of the award required the Royal Court to raise £7.6m in partnership funding. The building has been completed thanks to the generous support of those listed below.

We are particularly grateful for the contributions of over 5,700 audience members.

Royal Court Registered Charity number 231242.

THE AMERICAN FRIENDS OF THE ROYAL COURT THEATRE

AFRCT support the mission of the Royal Court and are primarily focused on raising funds to enable the theatre to produce new work by emerging American writers. Since this not-for-profit organisation was founded in 1997, AFRCT has contributed to seven productions including Rebecca Gilman's Spinning Into Butter. They have also supported the participation of young artists in the Royal Court's acclaimed International Residency.

If you would like to support the ongoing work of the Royal Court, please contact the Development Department on 020 7565 5050.

THE ARTS COUNCIL OF ENGLAND

PROGRAMME SUPPORTERS

The Royal Court (English Stage Company Ltd) receives its principal funding from London Arts. It is also supported financially by a wide range of private companies and public bodies and earns the remainder of its income from the box office and its own trading activities.

The Royal Borough of Kensington & Chelsea gives an annual grant to the Royal Court Young Writers' Programme and the London Boroughs Grants Committee provides project funding for a number of play development initiatives.

The Jerwood Charitable Foundation continues to support new plays by new playwrights with the series of Jerwood New Playwrights. Since 1993 the A.S.K. Theater Projects of Los Angeles has funded a Playwrights' Programme at the theatre. Bloomberg Mondays, a continuation of the Royal Court's reduced price ticket scheme, is supported by Bloomberg.

Sky has also generously committed to a two-year sponsorship of the Royal Court Young Writers' Festival.

LONDON ARTS

AWARDS FOR
THE ROYAL COURT

Terry Johnson's Hysteria won the 1994 Olivier Award for Best Comedy, and also the Writers' Guild Award for Best West End Play. Kevin Elyot's My Night with Reg won the 1994 Writers' Guild Award for Best Fringe Play, the Evening Standard Award for Best Comedy, and the 1994 Olivier Award for Best Comedy. Joe Penhall was joint winner of the 1994 John Whiting Award for Some Voices. Sebastian Barry won the 1995 Writers' Guild Award for Best Fringe Play, the 1995 Critics' Circle Award and the 1997 Christopher Ewart-Biggs Literary Prize for The Steward of Christendom, and the 1995 Lloyds Private Banking Playwright of the Year Award. Jez Butterworth won the 1995 George Devine Award for Most Promising Playwright, the 1995 Writers' Guild New Writer of the Year Award, the Evening Standard Award for Most Promising Playwright and the 1995 Olivier Award for Best Comedy for Mojo.

The Royal Court won the 1995 Prudential Award for Theatre and was the overall winner of the 1995 Prudential Award for the Arts for creativity, excellence, innovation and accessibility. The Royal Court Theatre Upstairs won the 1995 Peter Brook Empty Space Award for innovation and excellence in theatre.

Michael Wynne won the 1996 Meyer-Whitworth Award for The Knocky. Martin McDonagh won the 1996 George Devine Award, the 1996 Writers' Guild Best Fringe Play Award, the 1996 Critics' Circle Award and the 1996 Evening Standard Award for Most Promising Playwright for The Beauty Queen of Leenane. Marina Carr won the 19th Susan Smith Blackburn Prize (1996/7) for Portia Coughlan. Conor McPherson won the 1997 George Devine Award, the 1997 Critics' Circle Award and the 1997 Evening Standard Award for Most Promising Playwright for The Weir. Ayub Khan-Din won the 1997 Writers' Guild Award for Best West End Play, the 1997 Writers' Guild New Writer of the Year Award and the 1996 John Whiting Award for East is East. Anthony Neilson won the 1997 Writers' Guild Award for Best Fringe Play for The Censor.

At the 1998 Tony Awards, Martin McDonagh's The Beauty Queen of Leenane (co-production with Druid Theatre Company) won four awards including Garry Hynes for Best Director and was nominated for a further two. Eugene Ionesco's The Chairs (co-production with Theatre de Complicite) was nominated for six Tony awards. David Hare won the 1998 Time Out Live Award for Outstanding Achievement and six awards in New York including the Drama League, Drama Desk and New York Critics Circle Award for Via Dolorosa. Sarah Kane won the 1998 Arts Foundation Fellowship in Playwriting. Rebecca Prichard won the 1998 Critics' Circle Award for Most Promising Playwright for Yard Gal (co-production with Clean Break).

Conor McPherson won the 1999 Olivier Award for Best New Play for The Weir. The Royal Court won the 1999 ITI Award for Excellence in International Theatre. Sarah Kane's Cleansed was judged Best Foreign Language Play in 1999 by Theater Heute in Germany. Gary Mitchell won the 1999 Pearson Best Play Award for Trust. Rebecca Gilman was joint winner of the 1999 George Devine Award and won the 1999 Evening Standard Award for Most Promising Playwright for The Glory of Living.

Roy Williams and Gary Mitchell were joint winners of the George Devine Award 2000 for Most Promising Playwright for Lift Off and The Force of Change respectively. At the Barclays Theatre Awards 2000 presented by the TMA, Richard Wilson won the Best Director Award for David Gieselmann's Mr Kolpert and Jeremy Herbert won the Best Designer Award for Sarah Kane's 4.48 Psychosis. Gary Mitchell won the Evening Standard's Charles Wintour Award 2000 for Most Promising Playwright for The Force of Change. Stephen Jeffreys' I Just Stopped by to See The Man won an AT&T: On Stage Award 2000. David Eldridge's Under the Blue Sky won the Time Out Live Award 2001 for Best New Play in the West End.

In 1999, the Royal Court won the European theatre prize New Theatrical Realities, presented at Taormina Arte in Sicily, for its efforts in recent years in discovering and producing the work of young British dramatists.

ROYAL COURT BOOKSHOP

The bookshop offers a wide range of playtexts, theatre books, screenplays and art-house videos with over 1,000 titles. Located in the downstairs Bar and Food area, the bookshop is open Monday to Saturday, afternoons and evenings.

Many Royal Court playtexts are available for just £2 including the plays in the current season and recent works by David Hare, Conor McPherson, Martin Crimp, Sarah Kane, David Mamet, Gary Mitchell, Martin McDonagh, Ayub Khan Din, Jim Cartwright and Rebecca Prichard. We offer a 10% reduction to students on a range of titles.
Further information : 020 7565 5024

The Bush Theatre in association with the Traverse Theatre
presents the Traverse Theatre Company production of

Among Unbroken Hearts

by Henry Adam

25 April – 19 May

Life
Joy
Fear
Trust
Need
Love
Hope
Death
Loss

Ray got away years ago. Went South. Found a new way to live.
Now the prodigal son is coming back to where it all began.
"East Jesusville, County Hell, United States of Shit. Cool address eh?"

Box Office

020 7610 4224

The Bush Theatre
Shepherds Bush Green
London W12
www.bushtheatre.co.uk

"A breath of fresh air" The Herald

"Adam lays bare the frustrations of a generation" The Times

"Should be seen by as many people as possible, here and now" The Mail on Sunday

"The writing is first rate." The Guardian

"A truly impressive Traverse Debut from a dramatist full of skill and courage" The Scotsman

thebushtheatre

David Harrower
Presence

faber and faber

First published in 2001
by Faber and Faber Limited
3 Queen Square, London WC1N 3AU
First published in the United States in 2001 by Faber and Faber Inc.
an affiliate of Farrar, Straus and Giroux LLC, New York

Typeset by Country Setting, Kingsdown, Kent CT14 8ES
Printed in England by Mackays of Chatham plc, Chatham, Kent

© David Harrower, 2001

The right of David Harrower to be identified as author
of this work has been asserted in accordance with
Section 77 of the Copyright, Designs and Patents Act 1988

A CIP record for this book
is available from the British Library

ISBN 0–571–21059–7

2 4 6 8 10 9 7 5 3 1

For Gina Moxley

Characters

Paul
Pete
George
Marian
Elke

Hamburg, 1960

ONE

Dingy basement room. Paul and Pete throw themselves onto two beds, claiming them. George, the last in, stands looking at the sofa. All have a bag or small suitcase with them.

George Is this it? Should be a bed. Where's the bed? This's a sofa.

Paul Full marks, 'tis a sofa, yeah.

George A bloody sofa!

Paul Definitely. Sofa. Isn't it?

Pete Yeah.

George What's there only a sofa doing here? There should be a bed. That Bruno promised beds for all of us. One, two – where's three?

Paul Nowhere round here anyway, no.

George The bastard. The bastard.

Paul Through there you'll be. In with the two of them through there.

George 'Course, yeah. All right. See ya.

Paul See ya, yeah.

George leaves.

They can have him.

Silence. Paul moans with tiredness. George re-enters.

George That Bruno is a bastard! This's it. Them two've got two beds, nothing else. Fuck this. Sofa. Glad to see you lads've made yourselves comfortable.

Paul I'm utterly comfortable, thanks, yeah. You, Pete?

Pete Fine.

Paul Fine – thanks . . . Thank him for inquiring. He's concerned about us.

George Two months on this! Come'n feel this. Pete. Back inside the bloody womb here.

Paul Keep telling you you're too slow. You need to be quicker. You need to want things more.

George I'm not stampeding across a dark road, getting meself run over, crashing through doors, down a stinking corridor to fight over who gets a filthy bed.

Paul Shut the mouth and stop the complaining then. You deserve what you got. (*Pause.*) Go on. Say it.

George What?

Paul Face on you. You're about to say something. See that, Pete. The features all twisted like that – there's a thought coming. Say it then.

George He's only been with us six weeks. (*to Pete*) You've only been with us six weeks. I've been with us two and a half years. February 6th 1958. That gives me the right to have a bed, doesn't it? Pecking order and all that.

> Pause. Paul looks at Pete. Pause. Pete begins to get up
> from the bed.

Paul 'Course if it was me I'd stay where I was. If I got the bed fair and square first. Wouldn't go listening to any whining teenager.

George Ay . . . C'mon . . . He was nearly off there. (*to Paul*) Thanks, you. Look at the state of this. Degradation. Pure degradation.

Paul Don't say that word. Reminds me of home.

George I'm going home once I've had a sit down. First boat home. Bye-bye, lads. I'm not being treated like this. Bastard Bruno thinking I'm some kind of soft touch.

Paul They're perceptive, the Germans. Famed for it.

Pete Maybe it's a zed-bed.

George Y'what, ya bastard?

Paul There you go. Zed-bed. Maybe it is.

George That'll be it . . . (*George is on his feet, bending over to pull sofa open.*)

Paul A continental zed-bed. (*Pull.*) Folding out into a comfortable double mattress. (*Pull.*) Providing additional floor-space during daylight hours. (*Last, furious pull.*) No, think it's just a sofa. You were right first time.

George Never was a third bed. Bastard was lying. Don't believe this . . .

Paul Well, believe it. (*to Pete*) It'll all be forgotten, half an hour.

Pause.

Pete Some face that Bruno has on him, though, eh?

Paul Is right. Shouldn't be looking at anyone straight on, him. Without warning. The nose on him.

George The quiff on him.

Paul That's dangerous, that is. D'you see it wobbling? Thought the whole lot was going to come crashing down on us.

From the next room, the sound of a harmonica: 'Land of Hope and Glory'. Exaggerated mournful sound.

George Who's that?

Paul Winston. He nicked himself an harmonica in Arnhem. (*Shouts.*) Thievin' thief you are, Winston!

Loud, fast burst of 'Rule Britannia'.

That's more like it, son! (*Throws George a bottle of beer.*) Take that. Enjoy yourself. (*Raises his bottle.*) Hamburg. We got here.

George We are here, aren't we? We're bloody here!

Paul 'Course we are.

George All them lights on the streets lit up, this time of night. Everywhere open. And everywhere you bleedin' look, girls.

Paul Sitting in bars now, just waiting for us.

Pete None of them leaving early to take the last bus back home.

George None of them leaving early to take the last but one bus back home.

Paul Oh aye, lads, we're here. You can be certain of that. We're here.

George How we going to work it then? The first one of them I bring back here. How we going to work it?

Paul You stay clear of my bed for a start.

George C'mon, got to have a bed for that. Can't not have a bed for that.

Paul Sleep where we are. Sex where we are. Final.

George Who's going to sleep with me on this?

12

Paul Several hundred after tomorrow night. Queueing up, they'll be. Now listen. Rules. Anyone in here with a girl and sex's being had, the room's theirs for the duration, OK? Make the signal a . . . what?

Pete Sock.

Paul Perfect. Sock. Over the the door handle. The other two stay outside till it's over. Agreed?

Pete Agreed.

George That stinking corridor out there?

Paul Or go and get coffee or something, using their imagination or something.

George This's not a sofa any more, by the way. It's a bed. Any of you in here with a girl, there's no sitting on this, sweet-talking or necking, all right? 'Cause there's nowhere to sit in here any more. No sofa anywhere. Just three beds.

Paul Sweet-talking . . . We speak English. They don't. You only need to point at what you want, son.

George We going across the road then, take a look at this club Bruno has? Wander around a bit, see what's on offer?

Paul In a minute. We just got here. Let me finish this.

George (*shouts.*) How about you next door? You ready?

   No reply.

Who'd think the five of us were going to tear this city apart tomorrow night and leave it begging for more? They're out there waiting for us. They've been waiting all their lives. Well, I'm not going to disappoint them. (*He walks out.*)

   Pause.

Paul This's a tomb. They've put us in a tomb. We won't be seen again for a thousand years. They'll carry us out into the sunlight and the rays'll turn us into ash. Never identified.

Pete It's the oxygen, isn't it? That crumbles mummies?

Pause.

Paul Don't ever correct me again, all right? Or you're out on your arse.

Short pause. Pete looks across at Paul, who has his eyes shut, half-smile.

Pete Piss off.

Paul Very good, Pete. You're learning.

George re-enters.

George Brush the teeth first.

TWO

Club. Late night. Paul and George to one side, looking around the club. Both have been sweating heavily. A woman sits at a table with five bottles of beer on it.

Paul How many d'you make it?

George About twenty-odd. Definitely less than last night. Five left halfway through.

Paul Made their point, didn't they? We're up there sweating our balls off. (*Pause.*) Anything worth going after?

George There was a barmaid I saw . . . Ay, woman over there waving. (*Beat.*) No, no – old old old, don't look . . . You looked . . .

Paul It's her. Whatsername. Manages the place for Bruno. We met her last night, you daft get.

George It's dark in here.

Paul Does mean us, doesn't she? Yeah. Fuck. You're coming over with me, c'mon. And it's hello, thank you, then away. Don't get us snagged up with back home or families or whatever, OK?

They cross to Marian. She stands, shakes their hands.

Marian Good evening.

Paul Hello.

George Hello.

Marian Marian.

Paul Yeah. Marian. We remember.

Marian (*indicates bottles*) So please, these are for you.

Short pause. George takes one. Then Paul.

George Ta. Cheers.

Paul Cheers.

They drink. Paul still looking to get away quickly.

George The second night, eh?

Marian Yes. And number five of you, the drummer, where is he?

George On his way, I suppose.

Paul Doing his hair.

Marian *Wie?* I am sorry. I do not understand. You speak too fast.

Paul Nothing. Just an observation.

George Thing is, I've found this, we don't know we're speaking too fast, Marian. We all speak like this back home. My . . .

A look from Paul.

Yeah. So. Cheers again.

Marian Please. Do not stand. Sit.

Paul What it is, Marian, we have to go talk to the other lads now. All together.

Marian Ah, here is the fifth.

Pete enters.

Pete Hiya, Marian.

Marian Good evening. You will take a beer. And sit?

Paul No, we all of us have to talk, Marian. Team-talk, y'know? But see you later on though, eh?

George Thanks for the beer.

Marian I think the others, they are busy.

Paul Where?

Marian They are there. The bar. They speak with two of my barmaids.

Paul Yeah, see that now . . . There they are. Speaking away . . .

Marian I am sorry. We have only two barmaids. It is not enough, uh? So please, you will sit?

They sit.

Good. They do not speak much English, my girls. I think after short time there will be silence between them.

Paul Hope so. The walls in our room are as thin as paper.

George smirks.

Marian Again, I lose it.

Paul Pete, you want to explain?

Marian It does not matter. I must get used to it, no? (*Beat.*) So, I must tell you Bruno says sorry he is not with us. He is tonight at his other club. He is there most nights.

George So you're to be our gaffer then, Marian?

Marian To be your . . .

George Gaffer . . .?

Paul Foreman . . .

George Above us.

Paul He's saying he's under you, Marian, and you're on top of him . . .

George Ay . . .

Pete Boss, Marian. He's meaning you're the boss.

Marian Ah. *Bosse. Ja.* Yes. Boss. So you must do what I say, no? Gaffer. So Bruno is my 'gaffer'.

George That's it.

Pete It's very good, your English.

Marian Ah no. Enough, sometimes. Other times, no.

Paul No, it is good, he's right. Very good.

George Yeah.

Paul Tremendous. Very clear.

Marian Thank you very much.

Paul Sorry? Didn't get that. We can joke with the boss though, can't we? With the gaffer?

Marian Of course. But always you should tell me what the joke is.

Paul As long as you promise to laugh. Will you? Can you laugh?

Marian Yes, I laugh. Of course.

George We didn't think anyone'd speak English here. This being Germany and all.

Marian I learnt when I was perhaps your age. But language you must always speak, no? Or it . . . in the head. It dries. Like wood. The head becomes wood. You try to speak but the words have . . . *versteinert* . . . you know? Like the forest.

Pete Petrified?

Marian *Ja.* Petrified. *Versteinert.*

George Yeah. Suppose.

Paul (*to Pete*) Very good, son. (*Indicates George.*) Marian, you know more words than he does.

Marian Ah no. You joke with me now. (*Beat.*) So tonight is not a good audience.

George Telling me.

Marian Thirty-seven last night is better. For first night is not bad. But tonight, twenty-one. And talking during songs. And tables leaving. But it will get better.

Pete Only one table left.

Marian But at the front. Where others see. It is not good.

George Still mid-week though, isn't it? Mid-week . . .

Paul Not the weekend yet, Marian.

Marian The audience should come every night. Other clubs are full every night.

Paul They'll come, don't you worry.

Marian Of course they will. People will talk about the five handsome boys playing at the Indra Club and they will come to see. Now if you will excuse me, I tell some of the waiters to go home. There is not enough work tonight.

Pete The waiters – the truncheons on their belts. (*Motions.*) The big sticks. Why?

George To beat up mouthy lads chatting up barmaids, hopefully.

Marian Because we are a port. We have docks. Like your city has. And sailors come. And men who work on ships. After months on the sea, here to spend their money. They buy women, beer, so there are fights. That is why the sticks. They are something before the police come. To save lives, sometimes. This is what I wish to say to you. There are bars and clubs here you should not go to. I will tell you of the names. Be careful each of you. You most of all.

George Why me?

Marian You are the youngest, no?

George Well, yeah . . . I don't look me age though.

Marian At ten o'clock each night there is curfew. Under eighteen is not allowed in clubs at night.

George Nobody told me about that!

Marian But it is your birthday soon, that is right? Bruno say in a few weeks.

George Yeah . . . Few weeks, yeah . . .

Marian Then all will be fine. Now I say goodnight. Please finish the beer.

Marian leaves. Pause.

George She seems all right, eh?

Paul Pushover.

Pete Asking her if she can laugh . . .

Paul Just checking. (*Looks across club.*) Those barmaids've got closer. What the fuck are those bastards saying to them? (*Pause.*) D'you hear her? Not one word about the fuckin' music.

THREE

Mid-morning. Pete and Paul on their beds. George stands by the wall with a postcard he's trying to write. Paul and George's light-coloured stage jackets hang on nails in the wall. Pete's dark jacket is on a coat-hanger.

George What'm I supposed to write on this stupid thing? Eh?

Paul Who's it to?

George Me mum and dad. What d'you say?

Paul Don't know. How well d'you know them?

George C'mon, I need help here. Has to be short. And comforting.

Pete What's on the front?

George (*holds it up. Reads from back*) 'The historic port of Hamburg sits on the banks of the majestic River Elbe. The whole area pictured was destroyed in the Great Fire of 1842. Maybe that's why our women are so red-hot . . .'

Paul Enough there already, isn't there? That's an evening's reading for your lot.

Pete Doesn't say that . . .

George Does. Look. Ssh . . .! (*Listens at the wall.*) Definitely a girl you saw coming out the toilet? Not making it up so I'll stand here like a desperate get? Was it one of them barmaids?

Paul D'you never see things with your eyes, blind lad? The barmaids are history. This was some other girl, don't know who.

George Why's there no noise? I want some noises.

Pete They were busy most of the night. Resting now, should think.

George Didn't hear a thing. You should've woken me.

Paul Tried to. You were flat out. Unreachable. On the sofa that couldn't be slept on.

George (*returning to sofa*) Bed, not a sofa. Told you that. 'Hello, Mum. Hello, Dad.' Harold and Louise.

Paul How many postcards you got there?

George Four. And all taken. Me nan, me sister . . .

Paul I don't want any. Don't want to think about home. I want to think about being here. Want to think about getting out this fuckin' bunker. (*Pause.*) Money's crap. Accommodation's crap. There you go. The wind's a bastard. You taking this down? Everyone carries knives or sticks. Playing eight hours with one half-hour break to an average audience of ten. Thanks for letting me come to realise my dream. Wouldn't change places with anyone in the world right now. Love ya. Your deluded son, George.

George I *wouldn't* change places with anyone in the world right now. You wouldn't change places with anyone in the world right now.

Paul Yeah, I would. Them next door for a start.

George Not for me. Harold and Louise come first now. Hello, Mum. Hello, Dad . . . What d'you write yours?

Pete I'm not. I'm phoning them.

Paul Phoning them?

George Why?

Paul What's so important?

Pete Nothing. Just phoning them. They're me mum and dad.

Paul Much's that going to cost?

Pete Won't. Me mum said to transfer the charges.

George Did she? Mine never.

Pete Phone them. Won't cost much.

Paul Cost enough.

Pete Save you writing that.

George Nah, they bloody want a postcard, don't they? It's a bloody family event. First postcard I've ever sent them.

Pete The first? Ever?

George So?

Pete Never been away from home before?

George Prestatyn, yeah. Blackpool, yeah. But always with Harold and Louise. Never been away on me own before.

Pete And first place they let you come's here?

George Saying that like I'm nine years old!

Paul They knew I was coming, didn't they? Harold and Louise trust me for some reason I've never fathomed.

George Was brilliant, wasn't it? He was there. I just asked them straight out. Can I go?

Paul It's a once-in-a-lifetime experience, Louise.

George The apprenticeship'll still be there when I get back. And I'll have seen a bit of the world. Me mind'll be expanded. On you go, they said.

Paul The door frame gave way, didn't it, as they were pushing him out.

George Couple of months here and back in time to do me electrician exams, eh?

Paul You'll make a great electrician, you will. Oh, and the prospects for the future . . . Knocking on thousands of people's doors. Wiring up their bedside lamps. Reckon he'll still talk to us, couple of years time, Pete?

George Listen, it's a solid trade. I know things you don't. Look around this room, you can't see anything. When I look around it, I see it with electrician's eyes.

Paul Fuck does that mean?

George It's a deathtrap in here. You don't have a clue. The state of that wiring . . . That's a fire wanting to happen. Not waiting to happen, wanting to happen. Nine times out of ten fire starts when people are sleeping. Almost like it listens till we're off our guard. Judging the right moment to strike. The body unaware. I love fire. Always have. An electrician always knows it's there, over his shoulder, behind everything he does. Saw a charred body once. Went with me brothers – they're both electricians – to a house that'd burnt down. This bloke was sitting on the floor grinning. I wasn't supposed to see him. Looked like he'd enjoyed it happening to him. That was the best thing I ever saw, I think. He was there but he was gone. No eyes, no ears, no insides – they all liquify. His lips had burnt off. He's sitting there, grinning. Petrified . . . Petrified forest. That's what the house looked like. And how d'you think they get him out of there? They'd have had to snap his . . .

Paul All right, all right.

George Like charcoal.

Paul I wasn't listening, but I don't want to hear this.

George Just warning you.

Paul Do something about it then.

George Gives me one over you, doesn't it? When you wake up in the night and me bed's empty . . .

Pete stands up.

He's smart. He's getting out.

Pete I'm off to phone.

Paul now spots Pete's coat-hanger.

Paul Ay. Where'd you get the coat-hanger?

Pete From the management.

Paul You been fraternising with the management?

George Catching on to the lingo quick, isn't he? The management. Marian the management?

Pete Yeah . . .

George Ooh . . . So where's ours?

Pete Go ask her then.

George I like that. Eh? You only got one for yourself?

Short pause.

Pete Yeah. Yeah, I did. Didn't give any of you one thought whatsoever. I'm only out for what I can get for meself. D'you not know that?

Paul That's all right. Long as you're clear about it.

Pete I'll go ask her.

George How come you get the dark jacket anyway, we all have to wear light ones?

Pete 'Cause I wasn't with you when you got them, was I? Me mum made me it.

George Saint for a mum you have. Our lady of transferring the charges. Making up dark jackets.

Pete leaves.

We should all have the same coloured jackets. D'you not think?

Paul doesn't reply. George tries to write postcard again.

Doesn't say a lot, does he? Pete. Bloke of few words. Still getting used to us, suppose. Doesn't really need to say a lot though, does he?

Paul What d'you mean?

George He's a good-looking bastard, isn't he?

Paul Says who?

George You've seen the way girls look at him.

Paul How come he's not lying in bed with a girl then, like them two through there?

25

George 'Cause he can pick and choose, can't he? He can pick and choose whereas us, we'll go with anything. Them two, they'll go with anything. Only he hasn't picked and chosen yet.

Paul Picked and chosen . . . What're you talking about? And I don't go with anything.

George You go with anything.

Paul I pick and choose, thank you very much.

George Well, you never have much to choose from.

Paul Piss off. How can a bloke say another bloke's good-looking?

George I just did.

Paul For some fuckin' reason, I'm interested in this. One bloke thinks another bloke's good-looking. Using what yardstick?

George No yardstick.

Paul There must be a yardstick.

George Yardstick? Where's the fuckin' yardstick come from?

Paul The yardstick of if he's so good-looking you must want to fuck him from behind up the arse. The yardstick you must want to *use* to fuck him from behind up the arse.

George Fuck off, you.

Paul Good-looking, me arse.

George I just said it. Didn't mean anything.

Paul Well, mean something. When you say something, mean something. Helps the rest of us, y'know?

Pause.

George Hello, Mum. Hello, Dad. Paul's a cunt and I mean that most sincerely.

FOUR

Marian at her desk in her office. Paul and Pete at the door. The office is very bare.

Marian Come. I am sorry, it is too small.

Paul It's a cupboard, not an office.

Marian A cupboard, yes. Please sit. Sit.

Paul Woof, woof.

Marian Why do you . . . like a dog?

Paul Sit. You're always telling us to sit. That's what we say to dogs.

Marian I am sorry. I did not know.

Paul We can do other tricks, y'know. He'll roll over and beg if you say it strict enough.

Marian But you know that Germans, they love dogs. It is crazy. Like children. Sometimes more than children. I do not understand this. I do not like dogs. And I have no children. I am a strange German woman, I think.

Paul Bad manners to disagree with the boss, eh?

Marian You have come for your money, yes, not to talk about dogs. Only two?

Pete Don't know where the rest are. Thought they'd be here when money's being handed out.

*Marian takes keys, goes to a cabinet, unlocks it.
On the top shelf is a safety deposit box. Below it,*

*an old gramophone: doesn't look to have been
touched in a long time.*

Paul Thought they'd smell it. We'll take it for them, if
you want.

Marian No, I must give it to each of them. It is how I do
this. To make it right.

Paul Fair enough.

*The phone on Marian's desk rings. She takes the box
to the desk.*

Marian Hello? Hello. *Ja.*

*She turns away from Paul and Pete; doesn't speak
much, mostly nodding. Pete sees the gramophone,
goes to look closer at it.*

Pete Look at this. Some machine, eh?

Paul Dinosaur.

*Pete touches it. Marian turns, sees Pete, interrupts her
call.*

Marian Please. Leave it. It is old. It is broken.

Pete sits down. Marian to phone.

Es tut mir leid. (*Listens for some moments more,
puts phone down.*) I am sorry. This was another club
manager wanting information. He asks a woman in
a cupboard for information. So. Your wages. Six
performances at thirty Deutschmarks is one hundred
and eighty Deutschmarks. For you. For you.

Pete Thanks.

Marian Count if you wish. I will not be offended.

Paul (*counts it, getting to his feet*) All there. (*to Pete*)
C'mon, boy. Up!

Marian I speak by telephone this morning to your manager, Alan.

Paul What for?

Marian About the audience. He says hello to all of you. He asks me if you are . . . bringing the . . . roof down . . . ?

Pete The house. Bringing the house down.

Marian Yes. I did not understand. He explain to me – bringing the house down. But I have to tell him you are not. You are not bringing the house down.

Paul What'd he say to that?

Marian To give you more time. He did not seem worried. But he is not here in Hamburg. It has been one week already and every night the audience fall. Every night on the Reeperbahn they are queuing to buy tickets. But they do not come to our club. It is very difficult, no.

Paul It's not that difficult. Think they call it competition.

Marian It is your night off tonight, yes?

Paul Don't tell me. You want us to go round town pasting up posters?

Marian writes on a piece of paper, hands it to Pete.

Marian Tonight you will go here.

Pete The Kaiser . . . keller.

Marian The Kaiserkeller. The Kaiser's Cellar.

Paul And what's the Kaiser keep down there?

Pete This not Bruno's other club . . . ?

Marian Yes. There is a British group who play there. They have been in Hamburg three months and every night the club is full.

Pete You want us to go here tonight?

Marian You do not have to pay. It is free for you.

Paul To see how it's done, is that it? They'll show us how it's done . . .

Marian Yes. How it is done in Hamburg. How they make a show.

Short pause. Paul begins to leave.

Paul Pete, you staying or you coming?

Pete begins to get up.

Marian It is where you are, no?

Paul (*off*) Pete . . .!

Pete leaves.

FIVE

Bar Gemini. George carries beer to a table where Paul and Pete are sitting. A waitress, Elke, stops him. She has an American accent.

Elke Hey, buddy, you didn't order those from me.

George No . . .

Elke If you wanna sit at a window table, you gotta order beer from a waitress.

George Oh . . .

Elke You buy beer from the bar, you gotta drink it at the bar. Tables are waitress service only.

George Sorry. Didn't know that. I'm not from here.

Elke I can tell that. Now you collect your friends, move over to the bar, all right?

George All right. Sure. (*He walks over to them.*)

Pete What was she saying?

George D'you get a look at her? Fuckin' hell! She's American. Speaks English.

Paul Beer.

George We can't have these here.

Paul Y'what?

George House rules. Tables are waitress service only.

Paul Fuck off. Put them down.

George We're not allowed.

Paul Put me beer down, you. I'm not in the mood for this.

George We have to do what she says. C'mon.

Paul (*calls over to Elke*) Excuse me! Over here . . .!

George What you doing?

Elke comes over.

Elke Let me guess. You don't wanna move, right?

George No, we're just going . . .

Paul I have a problem here . . .

Elke Do I have a kind face? Do I look like I wanna listen? I'm a waitress. I'm dead inside. Nothing behind the eyes. You move to the bar, that's the end of it.

Paul We order from you we have to tip you every time you bring us a beer . . .

Elke Like a waitress is employed to.

Paul Leaving us less money to get drunk with on our only night off. A night we want to sit down at a table and get drunk. So can you not ignore some stupid rule for one night?

George Ay . . .

Elke That's how it works here, buddy. (*Beat.*) All right then. This's what I'll do. I'll go tell the head waiter. He'll drag you across that floor to the bar. Except he'll miss out the bar, kick you straight out the door. I know what I'd do.

Paul looks at her. Pete rises to his feet.

Pete C'mon . . .

Paul You should be on our side here, shouldn't you? America.

Elke Is that right?

Paul Yeah. It is. Our darkest hour, etc., etc. Took your time deciding, didn't you? How d'you end up here?

Elke Sorry, do I look like I need to tell anyone anything? Busting my insides keeping these secrets to myself?

George We love America.

Elke There's no better place on earth.

George Always thought that's what it'd be like.

Paul Let us drink these here, then, America. Please. Come on . . .

Pete Nobody's wanting the table.

George Me arms are aching, holding these.

Elke I gotta ignore the stupid rules for the sake of three . . . whatever you are . . .

George Bet you can't guess what we are . . .

Pete Sailors.

Elke Sailors? Right . . .

Paul Yeah. Sailors. On shore leave for one night only. We've been at sea for months. That's why the window table. To gaze upon Hamburg for one precious night.

George Historic Hamburg on the majestic banks of the River Elbe.

Elke You ain't sailors. Sailors on shore leave are like mad dogs. You ain't got their eyes. Or their desperation. I'd know if you were sailors.

George We're musicians. We are. Look at us. Hardly a penny to rub together.

Elke Where you playing?

Pete The Indra Club.

Elke Where's that?

George No wonder no one's coming. No one knows where the bloody place is!

Elke Stay there for now. I'm being good to you, remember that. The moment I say move, you move, all right?

George All right. Sure.

Elke goes.

Paul See, Pete. The features all twisted again. Words forming. Here we go.

George She is fuckin' fantastic!

Paul Fuckin' pain in the neck.

George Pain in me balls! And I saw her first. Sailors . . . Where'd that come from?

Pete Bar Gemini. Gemini's the Twins. Twin stars: Castor and Pollux. They're meant to protect sailors at sea.

George Is that right? That's good.

Paul Fool. He'll use that now.

George Why didn't you say that? Would've impressed her.

Pete I didn't want to impress her. You saw her first.

George He's all right, he is. You're all right, you. That's me evening made, seeing her. Who to thank for choosing here?

Paul (*holds up piece of paper*) Marian. This's top of her danger list. Bar Gemini. We should be in the Kaiser's Cellar really.

George Don't understand.

Pete Bruno's other club.

Paul Learning how to please an audience. Like we're some kind of cabaret band. (*Beat.*) He thinks we should be there, don't you?

Pete No. But maybe we should've taken a look.

Paul On you go. (*Pause.*) We've got nothing to learn from anyone. Fuckin' cheek she has. We are who we are. We do what we do. No one can touch us. You want to try repeating that to yourself, Pete, before you go to sleep in your bed. Y'know? If you want to catch up with the rest of us who know it by heart. (*Silence.*) I need more beer.

Pete I'll get it.

George I'll get it. Sit down. It's all right. (*His hand goes up.*) Excuse me. Come here.

Elke approaches table.

Elke You know what I don't get? That some guys seem to think I ain't heard it all before. That they're going to come out with something special. Something that ain't come out a hundred other guys' mouths. But on you go, do your best.

George Just want three more bottles of beer, please.

Elke My theory's junked. I apologise. The table's yours, gentlemen. Three beers.

Paul Shouldn't be selling this lad drink. D'you know how old he is?

George Ay . . .!

Elke Oh, I don't care how old someone is. I only want to know how young they can be. (*She smiles at George, walks off.*)

George Sweet Jesus . . . D'you see the smile? That means something, doesn't it? Definitely means something. I saw her first, all right?

Paul You can have her. You can try and have her. Don't think she'll go for the sofa, d'you? He'll sit here all night looking at her, then leave without saying anything.

George That was before. This is now. This is most certainly now.

He gets up, exits. Silence for a few moments. Paul watching Pete. Raises his bottle.

Paul Dogs. Who don't obey their masters.

SIX

*Pete and George in basement room. Pete reading. George
slowly shuffles cards. All three jackets now hang on
coat-hangers.*

Pete No.

George Haven't said a word. (*Pause.*) One game.

Pete You've taken enough money off me already.

George We won't play for money. Play for fun. Why
not?

Pete You're too good at it. You'll beat me again. What
fun's that?

George That's learning. The fun of learning. Learn how
to be better.

Pete (*holds up book*) I've got this. I'll learn from this.

George You can't learn from a book.

Pete I'll lend it you. It's called: 'Respecting other people's
wishes'.

George You're no fun, you are.

Pete I know.

George C'mon. One game.

*Pete ignores him. He starts to shuffle cards more
flashily.*

Pete Back in me bedroom with me kid brother here.
Going to stop doing that? I'm not playing.

George What'm I supposed to do?

Pete Find something. No more magazines left you can
draw penises on the photos?

36

Silence.

George D'you think it's true? There's one girl, the girl for you, the perfect girl, out there somewhere. Believe that?

Pete Think so, yeah.

George You found her yet?

Pete No. Almost. Thought she was. Turns out she wasn't.

George She's still out there, then. Miss Perfect. Somewhere. Undiscovered. (*Beat.*) Fuckin' Sutcliffe's in love.

Pete I know.

George Astrid. Says he's going to marry her. Says he knew the moment he saw her. There better be someone like that out there for me. Never happened in my family, sure of that. Me brothers, they're all married. But it's like they turned round and the wife was just there. Like she was always there. Don't think any of them ever said, 'She's the one.' Or the other way round – the wives thinking that about me brothers. Don't think it even happened to Harold and Louise.

Pete Might've. You don't know.

George No. I know my family. (*Beat.*) But guess what? Think it might've happened to me in that bar, y'know . . . The waitress. Not sure though. Y'know what I'm going to do? I'm going to go back there, ask her out.

Pete That's your first mistake.

George What?

Pete I'm going to ask that waitress out.

George Aw, don't! That's not fair . . . You got the bed, you fuckin' greedy . . .

Pete Hang on, hang on. I'm *going* to ask that waitress out. Future tense. You should've done it that night.

George Awh . . . Awh, I know. I know.

Pete I've *asked* that waitress out. That's what you should be telling me.

George Couldn't do it with both of yous there. Want to do it alone. Me own way. I'm going to ask her to come and see us. She won't say no to that, will she?

Pete I don't know. You'll have to tell her where the fuckin' club is, for a start.

George C'mon, you know about these things. Girls look at you all the time. There's a fair chance she might say yeah, isn't there? If she's not interested in you.

Pete She's not interested in me, tell you that.

George So . . .?

Pete So yeah, there's a fair chance she'll say yeah.

George Yesss . . . Thank you. I knew it. (*Pause.*) The night she comes can I wear your jacket?

Pete No.

George C'mon . . .

Pete It'll be too big for you.

George It won't.

Pete I'm bigger than you.

George It'll fit me. Honest. I'll make it fit me. Let me try it. C'mon . . . (*Goes to jacket, puts it on.*) It's not too big, is it? Doesn't feel too big. How's it look?

Pete All right. Fits you. Just.

George So can I wear it the night she comes?

Pete If you leave me in peace, yeah.

George I'll leave you in all the sweet meadow-fresh peace you want, mate.

Pete What'll I wear? Your jacket'll be far too small.

George Wear his. His'll fit you. He can wear mine.

Pete to Paul's jacket. It fits.

There you are. Perfect. Where's his tie? (*George starts looking in Paul's bag. Indicating Paul's bed*) Right go he had at you last night, didn't he? Your face . . .

Pete D'you not think we should've had a look?

George No.

Pete Liar.

George I'm not lying! We are who we are. Can't change that. And no one can touch us.

Pause.

Pete Wish there was a mirror in here.

George You looked in here?

Pete No. What'm I going to look in his bag for? It's his bag. Come away from it.

George Come and help me look. Where are they? There's none in here.

Pete None what?

George He hasn't got any. Underpants. Where are they?

Pete There must be.

George Telling you. There's none here. What's he done with them?

Pete There has to be.

> *They hear Paul's voice from the end of the corridor, outside. Pete pulls the jacket off, hangs it back up, jumps onto his bed. George moves back to the sofa, still wearing Pete's jacket. Paul enters, wearing a towel round his waist.*

Paul (*voice-over*) Ih-yi-ya. Ih-yi-ya. Fuckin' freezing out there! Fuckin' freezing! (*Enters.*) Fuckin' freezing in here! Ohh . . . (*to George*) What you doing in that?

George He's lending me it.

Paul What – to play cards in?

George For the night that waitress at the Gemini comes to see us.

Paul You never asked her.

George But I'm going to. I'm going to. And she's going to say yes.

> *Paul begins to search out clothes, shivering. George looks at Pete, snorts.*

Paul What?

George Nothing.

Paul What is it?

Pete Nothing.

Paul What is it? Tell me what it is.

George Ask him.

Pete You bastard. You started it.

Paul Ask me what? Ask me what?

George It's nothing, it's nothing. Honest.

Paul (*to George*) You got a question to ask, ask it. You got a question to ask, ask it.

George Your bag.

Paul What about me bag? What about me fuckin' bag?

George There's no underpants in it.

   Short pause.

Paul You were in me bag looking for me underpants?

George We couldn't find any. Where are they?

   Paul takes the towel off, revealing underpants.

Paul Here. Here they are.

George Where's the rest of them?

Paul This's it.

Pete One pair?

George You only brought one pair?

Paul Me alarm went off late. I was in a rush. I forgot to pack them. I've only got the ones I had on. Don't worry, me old fella's sending me some more over, all right?

Pete Why don't you just buy some more here?

Paul No.

George If your old fella's sending them they won't get here for weeks.

Pete Just go out and buy some here.

Paul No.

George Why not?

Paul I'm not wearing German underpants.

George Y'what?

Paul Simple as that. I'm not wearing Kraut underpants next to my skin. (*Beat.*) Would you?

SEVEN

Pete at the harbourfront. Marian enters.

Marian You are watching the ships?

Pete Wondering where they've come from. Where they're sailing to.

Marian They will sail all over the world. Perhaps even to your city. Where are the others?

Pete Lunch. Across there. It's a seaman's mission.

Marian I know it.

Pete Did you know a bloke from Liverpool runs it? Unbelievable. You can run but you can't hide.

Marian So thank God you are able to eat your British food.

Pete Cornflakes for breakfast, cornflakes for lunch. He gives us them cheap. Think he's taken pity on us. I couldn't face them again.

Marian *Seeluft.* Air from the sea. It is good for you.

Pete Yeah.

Marian I like the music you play.

Pete Thanks.

Marian I like to watch you. The . . . excitement. So confident. It is a pity others do not want to watch also. (*Pause.*) You are apart from the others, I think.

Pete What d'you mean? Apart from them?

Marian To me, yes. You are on your own.

Pete No, it's 'cause I'm new. I'm not one of them yet. They have to accept me, that's what it is.

Marian I did not mean this. You do not seem to be the same.

Pete looks at her. Short pause.

Pete No, we're all the same. Everyone from Liverpool's the same.

Pause.

Marian You have drunk a lot last night?

Short pause.

Pete Yeah. (*Pause.*) I read something on a postcard. 1842, the whole city was burnt to the ground. Is that right?

Marian The Great Fire of Hamburg. There was nothing left. It was truly terrible. The heat. I have never felt such heat. (*He looks at her.*) I joke with you. All of you think I am so old. No, I have seen it. How the young look at the old.

Pete You're not old. You're *older* but you're not old.

Marian I am old enough. I am the age I am. We shall leave it at that, yes? (*Pause.*) You did not go to the Kaiserkeller?

Short pause.

Pete No. We didn't.

Pause.

Marian You were angry with me. But as I said before,

43

you are in Hamburg. Do you want to stay in Hamburg?
Or is it why you come here, to look at ships? You would
like to be on a ship home?

Pete No, I want to stay. We want to stay.

Marian So you must want to have a good time. And
have many girls watching you.

Pete It'd help. Bit of adulation never harmed anyone.

Marian Bruno has said to me maybe we should have
two or three stripper girls again. But I do not agree. The
audience is tired now of stripper girls in clubs. They can
watch the girls in windows. It is music now they want
to see. British music. They want a show. Big. Loud.
You must be more exciting than stripper girls. You are
a handsome boy, Pete. You know this. Why do you not
go at the front?

Pete At the front?

Marian On the stage. Do you sing?

Pete No, I play the drums, Marian.

Marian I think maybe you should be at the front.

Pete You're joking, aren't you?

Marian I do not joke. I have seen girls when they watch
you. You are the one they look at.

Pete Hang on a minute. Hang on . . .

Marian It is only to think about.

Pete No. I'm not going to think about it. Stop talking
about it.

Marian It is a business. We must make money to
survive. (*She walks away.*)

EIGHT

Paul and George in Bar Gemini. Early hours of the morning.

Paul Don't know what I'm here for anyhow. Holding your hand.

George You're not holding me hand. Told you. Wouldn't have looked right if I'd come alone.

Paul Only one who needs to be here is you. And her.

George I was nervous, all right? But I'm fine now. I'll be fine. Be no bother. (*Pause.*) Marian hardly looked at us tonight, you see that?

Paul She'll be off crying to Bruno now. Telling him what arrogant cunts we are.

George Hope there's no trouble.

Paul Bruno liked what he heard. He liked what he saw. That's why he brought us over. We're not going to be dicked around by them. Here she comes.

George Is she? Fuck.

Paul Just take it easy. Be yourself. And let her know you know what you want.

George I don't need advice from you.

Paul (*getting up*) All right then.

George Where you going? Stay! It'll look too obvious. And in case I freeze.

Paul In case you what?

George Happens whenever I know I'm going to ask a girl out.

Elke enters with a bottle of beer. George freezes.

Elke Back again, huh?

Short pause.

Paul Yeah. Unwinding after a long night.

Elke You get many in tonight?

Paul glances at George.

Paul A few.

Pause.

Elke Just two of you tonight?

Paul Yeah. Just the two of us. Pete's stayed in. He's not used to our Olympian levels of drinking.

George Not disappointed, are you?

Elke Disappointed? No. Why would I be disappointed?

Paul (*cutting in*) I thought you're on your break?

Elke I am.

Paul What's that?

Elke Beer. We drink beer on our break.

George Do ya?

Paul Incredible, that is, isn't it? That'd never happen at home. Not in a million years.

Elke Gotta do something to keep us happy in this dump. Getting high for the graveyard shift usually does it.

Paul So why stay here? Why not go back to America?

Elke I ain't American.

George What are you?

Elke German.

Paul No, you're not.

Elke I'm German.

George You're American.

Elke America's where I wanna go. America's where I wanna be. I was raised in Berlin. The American sector? That's how come the accent. I've been working on it a couple of years now, getting it right. It's pretty good, huh?

George It's perfect.

Elke See, when I get to America I don't ever want to be asked about this shithole of a country again.

George Why? I love it here. I love this city. You want to see where I come from.

Elke You know what this city is? It's a dumping ground. It's a trash-can. All these people come here to dump their shit and spunk and vomit on us. And we stay open all night to let them do it. Because we know it's no more than we're worth.

Paul That's not why we came here.

Elke But you'd heard stories about how wild it was here. How anything goes?

Paul We'd heard stories, yeah.

Elke You can do things here you can't do anywhere else in Europe. And we want you to. 'Cause remember what country you're in.

Paul I remember.

Elke Your fathers must have fought us, right? Might even have been killed by us, right? But let's not talk about that. Let's drink beer and fuck women. Let's not bring any of that other stuff up. You're British. You're too polite for that.

Paul We're not British. We're from Liverpool.

Elke Let me tell you a secret. A secret everybody knows. The club you're playing in? I do know it. You know why? It's owned by a Nazi.

Silence.

George (*short laugh*) You're joking. Bruno?

Elke I don't know his name. You work for him. You should know his name.

George Bruno's his name.

Elke He's a Nazi.

Pause.

Paul Fuckin' hell!.

Elke Nobody told you?

Paul Nobody told us a thing.

George You sure?

Elke He wasn't SS or anything. The word is Panzer Division. Still makes him a Nazi. But it's 1960 and that's all right now. The Soviets are the evil race now. Don't matter there's hundreds of doctors, lawyers, greengrocers, club-owners in this city who are murderers. That's why I want to leave. That's why I want America. Every time I breathe in here I want to throw up. There's poison in the air. You not taste it? (*Pause. She gets up.*) You guys want another beer? Something to get rid of the taste?

Paul Yeah. Yeah, I do.

Elke I wish you were sailors. I'd stow away on your ship.

Paul Fuckin' hell!

George What about Marian?

Elke Who's Marian?

Pete enters.

Pete Don't look out the window.

Elke Shit . . .

Pete Police. Four of them. Coming this way.

George rises slowly to his feet.

George Fuck . . .! I got to get out.

Elke It's nothing to worry about.

Paul Yeah it is. He's under age. He shouldn't be here.

George Get me out of here!

NINE

Pete, George, Paul, Elke in an alleyway behind the bar.

George Which way?

Elke That way. That's the only way.

Pete That goes out to the front.

Elke It's the only way.

George I'm going to be caught. I'm going to be caught.

Paul Shut up. No, you're not.

Elke Stay against the wall where it's dark. At the end, look left. Two of them always wait outside. When they ain't looking, run.

George Fuckin' hell . . .!

Pete You coming or what?

Paul We should go one at a time.

Pete What – him first?

George I'm not going first!

Paul No. You.

Pete Why me?

Paul One of us has to go.

Pete Why not you?

Elke Somebody go, will ya?

Pete Fuckin' test, isn't it?

Elke Go!

George I'll go.

Paul No.

Pete Or d'you want me to get caught?

Paul No. We'd be fucked for tomorrow night, wouldn't we?

Elke You wanna go back inside and talk about this?

Pete goes. George looks at Paul.

George What was that for?

Paul Amusement. (*Beat.*) We have to be sure, don't we?

They wait, listen in silence. George is grinning.

Paul What you grinning at?

Elke I think he's made it.

Paul What you grinning at?

George I love this. I'm here right now. I'm right here. I'm nowhere else.

Paul What you on about?

George I wouldn't change places with anyone in the world. Everyone back at home's in their bed for work tomorrow morning. Look where I am. Look where we are.

Elke I like that philosophy.

Paul Knew you'd see sense.

George Thanks, mate. Seriously. Thanks for getting me here.

Paul You and your fuckin' apprenticeship. C'mon then. Start running. Or you'll be back changing plugs in three days' time.

George You go first. I'm fine. I'm enjoying this.

Elke For Christ's sake . . .!

Paul Strange lad, Elke. I accept no responsibility.

Paul goes. They wait, listen again.

George Feel invincible. Don't know why.

Elke I gotta go.

George Come and see us play tomorrow night.

Elke OK. Sure.

George We can have a drink after.

Elke Yeah. I got customers waiting. (*She goes.*)

George We'll have a drink after.

George stands in the alleyway, smiling to himself.

TEN

Pete, George, Paul in basement room. George in Pete's jacket, pacing around, excited.

George How's it look?

Pete All right, yeah.

George How many packing the place tonight, then? Don't know what to do with meself, that excited.

Paul enters.

Paul We're having a meeting after. All of us. Decide what we're going to do about this. All right?

George Yeah. We got to decide something.

Paul We will.

George C'mon then, get your jackets on.

Paul (*pointing at George's jacket*) Give us it over, then.

George gives him his jacket. Paul throws his over to Pete.

George Here we go. Ay. Look at this. (*Holds up a sock.*) The sock. Familiarise yourself with it, gents. Next time you see this it's wrapped round that door handle and you'll be drinking coffee in that coffee bar long into the night.

Paul Won't take that long, will it?

George Take as long as I want it to. I'll decide me own rhythm for a change.

He begins to twirl the sock around his head. Marian enters. Immediate silence.

Marian I have been told you were almost caught by the police last night.

Pause.

Paul Yeah. Almost.

George We got away. Didn't we?

Marian The three of you were in Bar Gemini. A bar I said you should not go to.

Paul Yeah, well, we thought since it was our night off we'd go wherever we wanted to go. Y'know?

Marian I know what Hamburg is like. This is why I tell you.

Paul How d'you know about the police, Marian?

Marian Waiters at one bar talk to other waiters. Bosses talk to other bosses.

Paul Nothing to do with you, then?

Marian What do you mean?

Paul The thought came into my head. Maybe they were tipped off, the fuzz. (*to Pete and George*) Either of you think of that?

Marian I do not understand.

Paul We're not getting a big enough audience for you. Maybe you're losing money. You want rid of us. You call the police . . .

Marian I did not call the police!

Paul We get sent home. The contract's broken. You save your money.

Marian I would not call the police! Who do you think I am?

Paul We don't know, Marian. We don't know who you are.

Marian You are unbelievable! You bring the danger to yourselves! I do not call the police!

Paul All right . . .

George Sorry, Marian. But we should be getting on now.

Marian Then go! Go! There are maybe ten audience there. Ten! Does this not even bother your own pride, playing to ten people? Do you not even care? (*to Pete*) You did not tell them what I say to you? At the harbour . . .

Pete (*realises*) No. No way.

Paul What?

Pete Nothing. (*He begins to leave.*)

Marian I said for you maybe to ask them.

George What?

Marian He looks the best. He should be at the front.

Pete This came from nowhere. She just said it.

Marian It is him the girls like. It is him they will pay to see.

Pete I told you I don't want to hear this again!

Marian But I think it is a solution . . .

Pete walks out.

I am still speaking to you . . .

She turns, looks at Paul and George. They walk past her out of the room.

ELEVEN

Club. After the set. Paul sits, sweating, three bottles of beer in front of him. George enters, stops, looks at him.

Paul Quiet moment to meself.

George Don't believe you sometimes.

Paul Hard to, isn't it?

George Could've given us some warning. Fuckin' hell.

Paul Just came out me mouth, didn't it?

George Straight into the microphone . . .

Paul Happens sometimes. When you're furious. When you're getting dicked about. (*Pause.*) So we get sacked . . .

George Without a fuckin' doubt, yeah.

Paul But she wasn't here, was she though?

George She'll hear about it. She knew about the Gemini, knew about the police. I'd say she'll get to know about this.

Paul Fuck it. I don't care. Fuck Bruno. Fuck Marian. Fuck this club. Fuck that fuckin' room we're in. (*Beat.*) See the audience's faces though? Electric shock right up their arse. Worth it for that. Where you going? Thought we were having a meeting.

George I've business to attend to. When I find the business.

Paul Ay. Where's Pete? Pete the traitor?

George shrugs.

Fletcher fuckin' Christian, the cunt.

George C'mon, should feel sorry for him. Marian the management wants the young lad, doesn't she?

Paul You'd better move fast then. He could be pulling the sock over the door handle as we speak.

George (*makes a face*) Awh . . . no.

   Elke enters.

Elke Found you. (*Begins to clap, focusing on Paul.*) That was something! Jesus Christ! Unbelievable.

Paul Someone appreciates me. Thanks.

Elke I thought I was dreaming it! 'We want to dedicate . . . '

George Aw don't . . .

Elke ' . . . our last song to all the Nazis in the audience.'

Paul 'Sieg heil, you bunch of bastards.'

Elke But you forgot the salute! When you say 'Sieg heil' you gotta do the salute! I was not expecting that.

George What about the music? Did you like that?

Elke It was great, yeah. Yeah . . . You do that every night? At the end.

Paul You've been priviliged to witness the first time.

George First and only time. The last time.

Elke Hell, you'll find another club.

George The crowd-pleasers that we are.

Elke I know some people, don't worry. Can I get a beer? Boy, I need one.

Paul On you go.

George I'll take you to the bar, Elke, buy you one.

Elke I'm fine now. Yeah, I know people. They'll fix you up. I'll show you how to salute as well.

Paul Was all his idea, y'know.

George It was not.

Paul Take the credit, go on.

George It wasn't me. Shut up. Go get some more beer in.

Paul I got these!

George holding out money.

Oh, yeah. Right. Beer again, then. Not back in ten minutes I've been rounded up.

Paul goes. Pause. Elke looks off in direction Paul went.

George Go somewhere else in a bit, eh? Get out of here.

Elke Sure, yeah. Good idea.

George Great.

Pause. Lengthening.

Ay. Bar Gemini. And Gemini's the Twins, isn't it?

Elke Yeah.

George The Twins, yeah. I used to know their names but I've forgotten them. They looked after sailors apparently. (*Beat.*) You could get the two of them for the price of one . . .

Elke doesn't laugh.

Be why the bar's called that, is it? 'Cause it's near the docks with all the ships and sailors and that . . .

Elke I think it's 'cause you gotta be schizophrenic to work there. (*She drains her beer.*) That's me done.

She stands up. George hurriedly trying to drink his beer.

George Hang on a mo'. Hang on . . .

She begins to walk away.

Elke I'll go get Paul.

George stops, looks at her.

I know a secret bar no one knows about. It's a wild place. We'll meet you out front, say ten minutes, OK?

She goes. George stares ahead of him, then after a moment walks out in opposite direction.

TWELVE

Basement room. Two candles lit. Pete lies on his bed, staring at the ceiling. George enters. They look at each other.

George And don't think I'm speaking to you, you traitorous bastard.

Paul Where's traitor come from? I told you already . . .

George I couldn't give a fuck . . . Fletcher fuckin' Christian.

Paul She just came out with it! Was nothing to do with me. I'd no idea she was going to say it.

George I'm not listening. You can fuckin' have this back.

He takes Pete's jacket off, throws it onto the floor near him. Pete looks at him, gets up, picks up jacket,

58

hangs it back on the wall. While he does this, George looks at the bed, walks over to it, lies down.

George And I'll have this, seeing as I deserve it.

Pete goes to sofa, sits. Silence.

Pete This 'cause of what he said?

George 'Sieg heil'? No, I thought that was fuckin' hilarious. Fuckin' hilarious.

Pause.

Pete Where's Elke?

Pause.

George She's in some bar with him. I asked her out and he's sitting in some dark corner with her.

Pete Oh.

George Yeah, 'Oh'. And leave it at that. Sat in that coffee bar across the road, five cups of coffee. I don't even drink coffee. (*Pause.*) Wasn't speaking to you and you've got me chatting away already. See, you're sly as well, you are, Best. Can't be trusted an inch. I was the one fuckin' asked her out.

Pete Oh well. As me mum says, 'Wait and see what the morning brings.'

George It's bringing death. I'm going to murder both of you in your beds. I'm going to murder you in your fuckin' sofa. (*Pause.*) Finally got the bed, can't even fuckin' sleep. If me mum and dad could hear me fuckin' language. (*Pause.*) I don't want to go home yet. Be back before me fuckin' postcard. Don't know if I want to stay now either . . . (*Pause.*) It's that word. That fuckin' word . . .

Pete What word? What word? (*Pause.*) Nazi?

George Something about it. When I hear it. Me mind just goes . . . numb. I can't think right. It doesn't . . . mean anything. I can't get it to mean anything. Or what it means is so . . . I don't know. Start feeling sick if I think about it too much.

Pete You have nightmares about them too when you were a kid? Men in black uniforms shooting babies.

George Me dad used to say, you behave or they'll come and get you. They'll put you in an oven. Fuckin' terrible thing to say to a kid.

Pete D'you remember when Hitler died?

George Too young. Cyanide, wasn't it? Him and Eva.

Pete Cyanide, then one of his men stabbed him. So it'd look like a soldier's death, not a coward's.

George Bastard. He was a coward.

Pete 'Course it wasn't him. It was a double. He's still alive somewhere.

George No, he's fuckin' not!

Pete He's just waiting for the right time. Then he'll be back.

George Fuck off.

Pete Ay, he could be Bruno – Adolf. Escaped to South America, plastic surgery, back here and bought this place. You've seen Bruno's face. Looks like it's been carved up by knives, don't it? Maybe he's Bruno.

George That'd just finish it for us, wouldn't it? Hello, Harold. Hello, Louise. Guess what? We're Adolf Hitler's in-house band. (*Pause.*) How could anyone support an evil, ugly cunt like that?

Silence. Paul enters, takes in the scene.

Paul Very romantic. Didn't mean to barge in, but there's no sock on the door.

George Fuck off, you. Where've you been? Eh? Where've you been?

Paul 'Mam? Mam? What're you doing here? You're so far from home . . . ' In a bar pouring beer down me neck.

George A little secret, wild bar somewhere?

Paul Y'what? We waited for you outside but you'd fuckin' disappeared.

George So the two of you fucked off to this bar . . .

Paul 'Cause we wanted to drink, yeah. Jesus Christ, what'm I supposed to do?

George Show some fuckin' loyalty.

Paul Wait around till you decide what you're going to do? I can't help you with everything, son. You should've got her back here and fucked her, like we all were told was going to happen.

George That what you did with her then? Is that what you did?

Paul I did nothing with her.

George Don't believe it.

Paul I don't fuckin' care. I want to sleep.

George Yeah, long train journey ahead of us, fuckin' thanks to you.

Paul We'll be back up on that stage tomorrow night, don't you worry. (*Silence.*) Oi, you. Fletcher fuckin' Christian, you mutinous bastard. Don't think I've forgotten about you. Sing us a lullaby, will you? C'mon, son. To help me get to sleep. C'mon. Come up to the front and let's hear your voice.

George Will you just give me some fuckin' peace!

Paul But we're having the time of our lives here.

THIRTEEN

Pete at the harbour. Elke has just entered, carrying a plastic bag.

Elke You're somewhere else. You ain't here.

Pete No, I'm here. I know that much.

Elke There's my escape route. The river into the sea. Then America the Beautiful.

Pete You're sailing to America?

Elke Cheapest way. And 'cause I wanna stand at the front of the ship as it leaves the harbour. I want everyone in this country to see me turning my back on it.

Pete Where're you going to go?

Elke Maybe I'll give Peter Lorre a call. Or Marlene. Maybe she's got a room to rent. I don't know. I don't know anybody there. But I'll end up somewhere, doing something. I always do. What do you think of Ellie?

Pete Who's Ellie?

Elke My new name. Or Elizabeth? Eleanor? Good for America. Eleanora? More mystery. Eve. Hey, I just thought of that. Eve. I like that. Eve. And round my American garden I'll build a white picket fence. (*Pause.*) You don't understand it. Me wanting to get out. The hatred I got.

Pete Never met anyone like you before, that's all.

Elke You don't feel the same, looking at all this? This shining new city? Bet you Liverpool don't look like this.

Pete Nothing like it.

Elke So what are you thinking? Something ain't right about this. How come we got everything you ain't got? (*Pause.*) You know what happened here, Pete? Eighteen years ago. August 1942.

Pete Yeah. I know what happened. The firebombing. I know about it.

Elke Day and night for nine days. Fifty thousand citizens of Hamburg dead. And it still didn't stop Hitler. The fire was a thousand degrees. Human fat was running in the gutters. Nobody'd guess now, would they? I guess that's the point. (*Pause.*) If you wanna say things, say them. If you got questions you wanna ask, ask them.

Pete I don't know what it is I want to hear.

Elke Just look them in the eye and ask.

Pete Bruno . . . Is it true?

Elke Yeah.

Pete Fuckin' hell. That feels fuckin' strange.

Elke But ask other people. And keep asking till someone gives you an answer. I gotta go find Paul. Hey, I gotta show you what I bought. (*From the bag, she brings out a pair of Nazi jackboots.*) What do you think? Got them in a junk shop. Beautiful, ain't they?

Pete What're they for? What d'you get them for?

Elke Paul.

Pete No. Elke . . .

She puts the boots back in the bag.

Elke He'll look fantastic in them. They're used, but we can shine them up.

Pete Don't. Please. Don't. I'm asking you.

Elke Why not?

Pete He's gone far enough, hasn't he?

Marian enters. Stands to one side, looking at them.

Elke There is no far enough! Who's it going to offend, Pete? Only those who should be offended. Do you think I'm some kind of naughty kid who's gone too far? Don't fucking think of me like that, OK? Don't fucking think of me like that.

Pause. Pete notices Marian. Elke turns to look.

Who are you?

Marian I am Marian. I am manager of the Indra Club. (*to Pete*) Can I speak with you?

Elke I'm going. Hey, maybe you can help me.

Marian I will try . . .

Elke I bought this pair of boots but I don't know if . . . (*She reaches into the bag.*) What do you think?

Marian I am sorry. I do not . . .

Pete Elke, no.

Elke looks at him for a moment, then pulls one of the jackboots out and holds it up.

Elke What do you think?

Marian says nothing. Pete can't help but look at her, for her reaction.

Not your style, huh? Where did you find these guys? They're incredible.

Elke exits. Pause.

Marian What is this?

Pete I don't know.

Marian I do not understand. Why does she have these things?

Pete turns back, to look out towards the river. Silence. Marian seems totally thrown by what's happened. She continues to look at Pete's back. A few moments pass.

I want to say I am sorry for what I said a few nights ago. In front of the others. I should not have said it. (*She goes.*)

FOURTEEN

The Indra. Busy. Elke waits, her coat beside her. Table has several unopened bottles of beer on it. Paul enters, wearing the jackboots. Raises his arms in triumph.

Paul Look at it! Look at this! They fuckin' love it! They fuckin' love us!

Elke You were incredible, that's why.

Paul Can't hear you. Too busy in here. Say it again.

Elke You were fucking incredible. And John saluted!

Paul I know. This's how it's meant to feel. About fuckin' time. And these . . . (*jackboots*) Genius. We need them for all of us. What's going on here? Whose are these? (*bottles*)

Elke They're for you. From your public. I told you it'd be like this.

Paul You did. You fuckin' did, didn't you? Should've listened to you all along.

They kiss. For a long time.

Elke And tomorrow there'll be more people. And more after that. Everyone in Hamburg will want to see you.

Paul You want to go back to me room?

Elke I can't tonight. I've got a shift starting ten minutes ago. But I got tomorrow night off.

Paul So have I. (*Kiss.*) I can just about wait till then.

Pete walks by.

Ay! Over here! Free beer!

Pete comes over.

From our adoring public. We're on top of the fuckin' world tonight. Go on.

Pete Don't want one. Don't feel like drinking.

Paul What's up with you? Enjoy yourself. Remember what that means?

Pete Was Marian here?

Elke Marian left. Wham. Soon as you guys ended she was gone. What does that tell you?

Paul She'll have legged it off to tell Bruno. Fuck her. Fuck both of them. We're going out on a high.

Elke It was fucking perfect. Better than last night. You are a showman.

Paul The boots gave it a little something extra, not think, Pete?

Pete I think tomorrow morning we pack our bags.

Paul Pay-day tomorrow. Show down. Paid first, then we pack our bags. Then Elke's going to find us another club.

Elke I gotta go to work. (*She gets up from table, puts her coat on.*)

Paul Where's the rest of them? We should be celebrating. Where's soft lad?

Pete Think he's gone back to the room.

Paul What the fuck for?

Elke leans down, kisses Paul, goes.

Pete I want you to stop.

Paul Stop what?

Pete You know what. (*Pause.*) It's not just me.

Paul Who else?

Pete George. (*Pause.*) It scares him.

Paul Scares him? Does it?

Pete Yes.

Paul Can he not come and tell me himself? Scares him . . .? (*He goes silent.*) All right. I hear you.

FIFTEEN

Day. Marian's office. The gramophone is on a table now, in full view. Pete enters, waits. Wanders over to the gramophone, looks at it, then sits. Paul enters with George. Pause.

Paul Where is she?

Pete Dunno.

Silence. They wait. Paul goes to gramophone.

Paul What's she got this out for?

George She should be here. I want my money.

Paul (*looks at record*) Benny fuckin' Goodman!

Short pause.

George And you, doesn't scare me, all right? I can speak for my fuckin' self.

Silence. Paul picks up the needle arm, the record turns.

Paul Thought she said this wasn't working.

He lifts the arm over. Music starts. Swing music from the 1930s.

George That's my dad's fuckin' music. Turn it off!

Paul Fuckin' awful, isn't it?

George Get it off!

Music stops.

Can't stand that fuckin' stuff.

Marian enters. Pause. They all look at her.

Marian Please do not touch that.

Paul We've come for our money.

Marian Of course. (*Marian to cupboard, brings out deposit box.*) You please sign here. One hundred and eighty deutschmarks. For you. For you. For you.

George Ta.

Marian Tonight is your free night, yes? Enjoy yourselves.

Marian returns box to cupboard. Paul is disconcerted. George moves to the door. Marian turns, faces them again.

Pete So what's happening here?

Marian What is happening?

Paul Yeah.

Marian Nothing is happening.

Paul What about Bruno? What did Bruno tell you to do?

Marian I have not spoken to Bruno. Bruno will not care. He will be happy now more people come to the club. You make money for him now.

Pete Tell me you're joking.

Paul (*grins*) She's not. She's fuckin' not.

Pete I don't believe this.

Marian If Bruno hears about what you are doing I will tell him it is what young people do. They get angry. They shout. Most often they do not even know why they do it.

Paul I know why I'm doing it.

Marian Do you?

Paul Yeah. So do you. (*Pause.*) Tell us. Tell us why we're doing it.

Marian I do not think you need to know more.

Paul Well, I think we do.

Marian You do not deserve to know.

George Deserve to know?

Paul Ay, we're employed by you. I think we've a right to know if our employers are . . .

Marian And what would you do then? (*Pause.*) We are told we must always explain to the young. We must always remind them so they will never forget. But the young must want to listen. But they do not.

Paul I'm listening.

George So am I.

Marian Go on shouting. That is what you want to do. This is how you want applause, girls. This is really what you want. You are young. You are stupid. You do not think about anything. Please leave my office now. Leave me. Leave!

They go. Marian is still for a time, then goes to the gramophone. She stands, looking at it. She turns. Pete is in the doorway.

Benny Goodman. We danced to Benny Goodman in clubs, when we were your age. I loved his music. I loved swing music. All of us would wear swing clothes and our hair, long. To here. (*Pause.*) The authorities forbid it. The Nazis. It was Jew music. Negro music. It was dirty. It would poison us. But still we went to to hear this poison. We were young. We would not be told what to do by anyone. They took us away. Maybe forty of us. To Moringen. It is a concentration camp. For youth. There were young people from all over Germany there. For five years I was in this camp. You wished to know. So how am I to you now?

Pause.

Pete Why are you here?

Marian Because it is my job. I must make money.

Pete What about Bruno . . . ?

Marian I do not know about Bruno.

Pete You must've . . .

Marian I do not want to know. What does it do for me to know? Who do I go to tell them this?

Pete But the things he might've done . . .

Marian I know some of these things. I do not need to guess. When they released me I did nothing. I said nothing. It is not only him to accuse. (*Pause.*) Why I am here . . .? Where else could I go? What other place?

SIXTEEN

Pete in coffee bar. George enters with cup of coffee.

George All right?

Pete Not great, no.

George 'Long you been here?

Pete Hour. (*Pause.*) D'you see the sock on the door?

George (*nods*) Be who I think it is, is it? Not bothered, like. She was never the one for me anyway. (*Pause.*) What'd you do today?

Pete Nothing much. Wandered around.

George Same here. Strange day, eh?

Pete Fuckin' right. Not sacked. Still here, still playing. I don't know what the fuck's going on.

George It's going to start getting good now, telling you. (*Pause.*) He'll stop doing it. Paul. I know him. He'll get bored of it. (*Pause.*) I'm not now but I got dead sad today. For about half an hour, dead sad. For home. For me mum and dad. 'Cause I thought – that's them cut for ever, isn't it? The ties that bind or whatever they're called. The apron strings. That's them severed. I'm not one of them any more. Can you say that about

71

your family? I'm not one of them any more. But I'm saying it, aren't I? I'm saying it now. I'm not one of them any more. And it's all right. (*Pause.*) How long d'you think he's going to be? Fuckin' ages, eh? They've started early enough. It's not even seven. (*Pause.*) I wanted in there to change me shirt. Change into a new shirt, y'know?

Pete looks at him.

You won't believe it.

Pete What?

George Told you. Strange day. I'm going on a date. Some girl fuckin' recognised me, didn't she? Came up to me on the street. She saw us last night. She saw me last night. Then she asked me out. Like that. Want to go out? So I said I'd think about it. Like fuck I did. I'm taking her out. Should be getting off now actually. Fuck the shirt. Looks like you'll be the last of us to get fucked, Pete. The best-looking of us. What kind of a fucked up country is this? Gives us all hope, doesn't it? I don't know what time I'll be back. Don't wait up.

George leaves.

SEVENTEEN

Basement room. Paul lies in bed. Candles lit. Pete enters, goes to sofa, begins to pack.

Paul Sorry 'bout that. Couldn't keep me hands off her.

Pete I've been sat in that café for five fuckin' hours.

Paul We had an agreement. You agreed to it. Anyhow, it's your night off. You should've gone out drinking. What're you doing?

72

Pete Packing. I'm leaving in the morning.

Paul Leaving?

Pete Yeah.

Paul You can't do that.

Pete If you're awake you can watch me.

Paul You've got fuck-all money.

Pete I'll start walking. I'll hitch-hike. I'm not staying here a day longer.

Short pause.

Paul And what about the rest of us?

Pete You can do what you want.

Paul No, you don't understand. We can't do without a drummer. If you go, we can't play. Then they really will sack us.

Pete I don't care.

Paul That's your problem, Pete. You should care about us.

Pete Fuck off.

Pause. Pete lies down on the sofa, to sleep. Paul continues to watch him.

Paul What'll you tell them back home? Back on your own?

Pause.

Pete It didn't work out.

Pause.

Paul 'Cause I'll tell them you up and left us. Deserted us. Ruined our chances just as we were getting going. That you can't be trusted one fuckin' inch. And you don't want that do you, Pete? Everyone back home knowing that. No one'll have you, will they? No one'll want you. (*Silence.*) So I'd unpack the bag if I was you. It's only six weeks more. And as soon as we're on British soil then we'll kick you out.

Silence. Paul blows out the candle nearest to him. After a moment, Pete crosses to Paul's bed, begins to drag him off it by his feet.

What the fuck you doing? Fuck off, you!

Pete You're sleeping on this fuckin' sofa! You're going to sleep on this fuckin' sofa!

Paul kicks out at Pete as he's pulled across the floor.

Paul Fuck off. Fuck off.

The light suddenly comes on. Both stop, look to the door. Marian is there, staring at them on the floor. They stare back at her.

What you doing here? Get out! Fuckin' knock!

She turns away. Paul up, grabbing at clothes.

You wanting the room for you and her, that it?

Marian It is George.

Paul What?

Marian The police have arrested him. He was out after the curfew.

Paul Fuck.

Marian This is why I warned you. You must take his things to him. Tonight they will hold him in the jail. Tomorrow morning he will be sent home.

Paul Nothing you can do, no?

Marian (*shakes her head*) The police also wish to talk with all of you. You must take your passports and papers. Bruno will be there. If you are the age you say you are then you are OK.

Paul packs George's bag – very quickly as there's little to pack.

Paul Got to feel sorry for the lad but we can do without him till we get back. Pete was going and all, Marian. But I managed to talk him round.

Paul leaves, taking George's bag. Pete gets up, takes his passport and papers from his bag.

Marian I do not like this boy. Not at all.

Pete Why don't you just sack us?

Marian It is not my decision.

Pete There's nothing I can do. I'm stuck here.

Marian Then you are like me. (*She looks at him, keeps looking.*) I have thought about you.

She moves towards him.

Pete Marian . . .

Pause.

Marian I am sorry.

Pete It's all right.

Marian I do not even know what I try to do.

Pete Yeah, you did.

Pause.

Marian If I was younger . . .

Pete Yeah. Maybe. (*He begins to leave.*) I'll see you tomorrow, I suppose. (*Short pause.*) I just want to go home, that's all.

Pete leaves. Marian stands for a moment, looking around the room. She picks up Pete's bag, then takes Paul's, pushing his clothes inside. Then she walks across to the single candle left lit. She picks it up and climbs onto the sofa. She holds the flame under the ceiling and with the carbon from the flame writes 'Pete Best'. She gets down and places the candle directly under where Pete's black jacket is hanging on the wall. She walks to the door, turns and looks. The black jacket begins to smoulder. She leaves. The jacket is in flames.

End.